Tales of A Modern Sage

Tales of A Modern Sage

STORIES OF THE FOUNDING MASTER OF WON BUDDHISM

Edited by Rev. Jeiwon Kim

Tales of a Modern Sage

Published by Won Dharma Publications
361 NY-23, Claverack, NY, 12513, USA
518-851-2581

Library of Congress Control Number: 2022917642

ISBN: 979-8-9869466-1-0

Illustration by Kim Sangyeop and Song Okjin
Cover Design by Kathy Abeyatunge

Printed in the Republic of Korea

This book is dedicated to the teachers who provide guidance for practitioners

in their search for truth along the Dharma path.

Contents

Part 2   Opening the Eye of the Wisdom

Part 3   Where Is the Awakened One?

Part 4 Searching for Truth

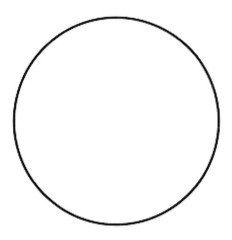

The origin of the universe

The true nature of all sentient beings

Editor's Foreword

On October 2, 2011, the opening ceremony for the Won Dharma Center was held in Claverack, NY. Many people gathered together to attend the dedication ceremony in celebration of that momentous occasion, which marked the beginning of Won Buddhism USA.

On that day, I spoke with other Won Buddhist ministers serving in North America who were working hard to spread the teachings of the Buddha in order to open people's minds and hearts. At that moment, an enormous sense of gratitude arose in my mind, and I felt called to do something that would support their efforts.

Thus, it occurred to me that it would be a great help to them if there were more books geared toward young western people to help facilitate their understanding of the teachings of the Buddha. In particular, I realized the necessity for a book to guide those who are new to Won Buddhism. This is how the idea to compile a selection of Sotaesan's tales was born.

This book is intended for young Americans as well as other western practitioners of any age so that they can joyfully read and easily grasp the essence of the Buddha's teachings.

All the stories contained in this book come from the collected memories of Won Buddhist ministers, various audio recordings, *The Scriptures of Won Buddhism*, and *The Anecdotes of Sotaesan* as well as *Dharma Words of That Time*. I would like to express my sincere gratitude to Rev. Seo Moonsung, who gave me permission to include and edit stories from his books. I am also thankful to Rev. Kim Sunghyun, who did the foundational work; Park Seonhee, the editor-in-chief; Han Jihoon, who wrote the first draft of the English translation; and Rev. Yoo Dosung, who painstakingly edited and polished the English translation by collecting the opinions of several American Won Buddhist members.

I also wish to extend my gratitude to the writers, Kim Sangyeop and Song Okjin, whose illustrations make this book more accessible and meaningful.

I sincerely hope and pray that through this book, many western practitioners will develop a deeper karmic tie and dharma affinity with the Buddha and Sotaesan. I further wish that in the near future, this book will be translated into many other languages, so it may brighten this world by opening the minds and hearts of all people and lead them toward the path of freedom.

May your everyday be a good day!

Rev. Bosan, Jeiwon Kim
Seoul, Korea
Winter, 2022

Translator's Foreword

The following true story happened many years ago in a suburb outside of Chicago. On a bitterly cold winter night, a woman boarded a train holding her baby bundled in blankets. The young mother, exhausted from travel, asked the conductor and a gentleman sitting next to her to wake her up when they reached her destination. Finally, after some time, the gentleman woke her, saying that her station was approaching. Quickly gathering her belongings, the woman holding her baby departed at the next station. A few hours later, the conductor approached the gentleman and inquired about the young mother. The gentleman said that she had gotten off at the previous station. The conductor panicked since that station had long been abandoned, and the train had just stopped there briefly for maintenance. After realizing they had been left at a closed station, the conductor stopped the train and raced to help the woman and baby. By the time they arrived, however, the woman and baby were already dead from the cold.

Why did the mother and her baby meet such a tragic end? The gentleman had no intention of harming her. To the contrary, he merely wanted to be of assistance. The issue was that the woman should have relied on the conductor, who was more familiar with the train's route and stations. She instead turned to the uninformed gentleman, who unknowingly provided her with the wrong information.

Throughout our lives we are surrounded by many people who love and care for us including our parents, partners, and friends. Like the aforementioned gentleman, these people mean well and are eager to lend a hand when necessary. Unfortunately, they do not always clearly know the path to liberation and eternal happiness. In truth, they themselves do not live completely free and contented lives.

We require an awakened teacher who clearly knows the Way as we navigate life, particularly when confronted with challenging circumstances. Only an awakened person with great wisdom can lead us along the right path. The Sanskrit name for Buddha translates to 'awakened one.' Those suffering and lost in a deep slumber can only be awakened by a Buddha, an awakened person.

This book is a collection of stories about the founder of Won Buddhism, Sotaesan. He is a new Buddha who was born in Korea in the late 19th century and came to this world to help ease the world's turmoil and free all beings from suffering. The reader will get a sense of how he spoke, acted, and lived through the ninety-nine stories shared from his life with his students. These stories serve as a beacon on our journey to freedom and happiness.

This world is entering a period of a profound awakening of consciousness. We must take advantage of this rare opportunity and devote our efforts to realizing the Truth to gain liberation from suffering.

We need to realize what a rare and magnificent gift it is to have met the buddhadharma. It would be comparable to throwing a needle into the air and having it land on a mustard seed.

Numerous people assisted me in translating *Tales of A Modern Sage* into English. I am grateful to Han Jihoon, who prepared the initial translation draft. Based on that work, many stories and sentences were edited and refined. I am also indebted to many Won Dharma Center members. Without their sincere and devoted assistance, this work would not have come to completion.

May all people be guided by the teachings of the buddhas, and may all sentient beings be free from suffering!

Rev. Dosung Yoo
Won Dharma Center, 2022

Cultivation of the mind for three days will last for a thousand years,
but material things amassed for a hundred years
will crumble into dust in one morning.

- Zen proverb

Introduction

Who is Sotaesan?

Sotaesan (1891-1943), the Founding Master of Won Buddhism, was enlightened to the Truth of Il-Won and established Won Buddhism in Korea.

Sotaesan was born in 1891 to a peasant family in a small South Korean rural village. At the age of seven, he began to have persistent questions about nature and the lives of the people around him. He wondered, "How high is the sky?" "Where do the clouds and wind come from?" He questioned everything he observed, and each inquiry led to the next. The more engrossed he became in these countless spiritual questions, the more frustrated he grew. He lacked spiritual guidance and was, therefore, unsure of what to do.

At the age of eleven, while attending a seasonal ceremony for the Remembrance of Ancestors, Sotaesan heard a story about an omniscient mountain spirit and hoped that meeting such a divine being would provide answers to all his spiritual questions. Every day for five years, Sotaesan walked four kilometers from his home to the Sambat Mountain Pass. For many years, he prayed to meet the mountain spirit, but he never did, which intensified his frustration.

Sotaesan heard an ancient tale at the age of sixteen about a person who had achieved enlightenment while practicing under a spiritual guide. After that, he spent the next six years looking for a spiritual guide who could help him find the answers he was seeking. However, he was unable to find one.

By the time Sotaesan was twenty-two, he stopped searching for a spiritual guide and instead became deeply absorbed with one single thought: "What am I supposed to do?"

During this time, he often entered deep meditation, forgetting time and place and resting in the genuine realm of stillness.

After twenty years of searching for the truth, on April 28th, 1916, Sotaesan's mind and heart opened to the ultimate reality, and all his questions melted away. He was twenty-six years old and had attained supreme enlightenment.

This day marks the beginning of Won Buddhism and is regarded as one of its most significant and auspicious events in its history.

After his enlightenment, Sotaesan read extensively from the scriptures of numerous religions. Upon reading the Diamond Sutra, he said, "Shakyamuni Buddha is truly the sage of sages. Although I have attained The Way without any teacher's guidance, looking back, from the time of my initial aspiration up to my final enlightenment, many aspects of my experience coincide with the practice and sayings of the Buddha in the past. For this reason, I adopt Shakyamuni Buddha as my original guide and the antecedent of my dharma. In the future, when I establish a religious order, I will create in this world a perfect and complete dharma by taking the teachings of the Buddha as its core."

Sotaesan embraced the Buddha's teaching but modernized and revitalized the traditional buddhadharma to make it relevant and accessible to as many people as possible to enrich their daily lives.

After his enlightenment, many people gathered to become his disciples and students. This newly created community organized a savings association under Sotaesan's direction. He said to his disciples, "For us to study and engage in spiritual practice, we must unite to generate income."

To make this a reality, each member made an effort to abstain from alcohol and smoking to save money for the larger cause. These efforts financially paved the way for establishing a community for spiritual practice.

Sotaesan then advised that they all purchase charcoal with the funds accrued from the members' savings, money borrowed from a wealthy neighbor, and Sotaesan's own money.

Due to the high demand for charcoal during World War I, the price of charcoal increased dramatically seven months later. As a result, the community savings association amassed a substantial fortune within one year.

Using the funds, in April 1918, Sotaesan and his followers constructed a levee on a deserted, muddy beach in his hometown of Youngsan. The levee kept the salty sea water at bay and those twenty-two acres eventually turned into fertile land. Crops were grown and sold to neighboring towns to provide a source of revenue and a means of subsistence for the developing Won Buddhist community.

In 1924, Sotaesan founded "The Society for the Study of Buddhadharma," a spiritual community with the mission of liberating all beings from suffering. This community flourished and later became the Headquarters of Won Buddhism, where Sotaesan and his followers worked, practiced, and studied the dharma under his new vision: "Daily life is buddhadharma and buddhadharma is daily life."

In 1943, after twenty-eight years of teaching, Sotaesan passed away at the age of 53.

Most scriptures from various spiritual traditions are transcriptions of oral transmissions. However, one of the distinguishing features of Won Buddhism is that Sotaesan wrote the Won Buddhist Scriptures himself. Until Sotaesan entered Nirvana, he meticulously edited and recorded his essential teachings, which are compiled in The Principal Book of Won Buddhism.

The rapid advancement of materialism and consumerism in contemporary society dominates people's minds, making them driven, competitive, and anxious. Material civilization itself is not the problem.

However, suppose the human mind and spirituality do not progress in tandem with material and technological advancements. In that case, a materialistic civilization can easily overwhelm us and become the primary source of suffering.

Sotaesan believed that the way to lead people to a happy life, free from suffering, is by empowering their minds and strengthening their spirituality. This can only be done through faith in truthful dharma and a realistic spiritual practice. That is why Won Buddhism emphasizes mind training practice.

Sotaesan, his self-created dharma title, literally means "cauldron," a traditional Korean cooker made of cast iron. This title represents his intention to provide spiritual sustenance to people from all walks of life.

What is Won Buddhism?

Won Buddhism is a reformed Buddhism founded by Master Sotaesan (1891-1943). It has transformed traditional Buddhist teachings into a more practical and approachable form. It aims to guide people in contemporary society by enriching their daily lives and providing a practical path to happiness.

After Sotaesan's great enlightenment, he created the image of Il-Won, also known as One Circle, which symbolizes ultimate reality. Il-Won represents the origin of the universe and our original nature. All Won Buddhist temples enshrine this Il-Won image at the altar as an object of faith and the model for practice in following Won Buddhist teachings.

Sotaesan observed that humanity was becoming dominated by the rapid development and advancement of material civilization. He then declared the founding motto of Won Buddhism: "With this Great Unfolding of material civilization, let there be a Great Unfolding of spirituality."

The central teaching of Won Buddhism is the Fourfold Grace, Dharmakaya (Truth) Buddha, which consists of the Grace of Heaven and Earth, the Grace of Parents, the Grace of Fellow Beings, and the Grace of Laws. The Fourfold Grace is fundamental to our efforts to transform this chaotic world into a peaceful one, as it expresses the interdependence of all beings. Scholars are increasingly incorporating the dharma of the Grace of Heaven and Earth into their attempts to address the current climate crisis.

In Won Buddhism, treating every living thing as a buddha is an act of faith, as expressed in the motto: "Everywhere a Buddha, Every Act a Buddha Offering."

Won Buddhism teaches us how to use our mind. Everything is of our mind's creation. This is the essence of the Buddha's teaching. Both the state of the world and the state of our lives are manifestations of our mind. Knowing how to use our mind is fundamental and is the key to a happy and fulfilling life. Therefore, mind practice, which teaches how to use the mind, is fundamental to Won Buddhist practice.

Timeless Meditation, Placeless Meditation is the essential path to mind practice, a way to practice meditation at all times, in every place. It teaches us how to maintain a peaceful, focused state of mind and how to use our original mind efficiently in our daily lives.

Through Sotaesan's vision, traditional buddhadharma was re-envisioned so that followers of Sotaesan could practice the path to enlightenment without abandoning their secular lives. Sotaesan emphasized that "Practitioners in the future should practice and work together to save both the body and the mind."

Won Buddhism welcomes and embraces all people and all traditions of other faiths and strives to establish a World of Oneness in which all people live in harmony. With its open and inclusive teachings, Won Buddhism is working to realize the vision of United Religions as a counterpart of the United Nations.

Part 1

LESSONS TO ENRICH OUR LIVES

1

About the Different Sages

When Cho Songgwang visited Sotaesan for the first time, Sotaesan said, "You seem to have qualities different from those of ordinary people. What is your faith?"

Songgwang replied, "I am an elder at a Protestant church and have been worshipping God for several decades."

Sotaesan said, "You say that you have worshiped God for several decades. So tell me, where is God."

"We say that God is omniscient, omnipotent, and omnipresent, so there is nowhere he does not exist."

"Then, do you regularly see Him, listen to His words, or receive His teachings?"

"So far, I have not seen or talked to Him."

"If that is the case, can you say that you are truly an intimate disciple of Jesus?"

"What shall I do to enable me to meet God and receive His teachings?"

"You may accomplish this by practicing with dedication and becoming a disciple who truly knows Jesus."

Songgwang asked again, "In the Bible, it is said that Jesus will return towards the end of the world and 'will come like a thief in the night,' but many signs of his return will appear at that time. Will there really be a day when He returns?"

Sotaesan said, "Sages are not deceitful. If you practice with dedication and your spiritual mind opens, then you will also understand Jesus' coming and going."

Songgwang replied, "I have been waiting for a long time for a great teacher who would give me personal guidance. Meeting you today, my mind is satisfied, and I would like to become your disciple right away. But at the same time, I have qualms of conscience because it seems like a betrayal of my faith."

Sotaesan said, "If a Christian becomes a disciple who truly knows Jesus, he will come also to understand what I am doing; and, if one becomes a disciple who truly understands me, he will come to understand what Jesus accomplished. Often people perceive gaps between different religions and become hostile to other religions. However, those with real understanding know that these religions have different names merely according to their time and place and come to view them all as belonging to a single household. It is important that you use your own discretion whether you stay or go."

Songgwang rose to his feet, bowed, and vowed anew to become his disciple. Sotaesan approved and said, "Even after you have become my disciple, you will be a true disciple of mine only when your own reverence for God grows stronger."

2

Worldly Pleasure vs Heavenly Pleasure

Sotaesan was visiting the agricultural department and after viewing very weak and skinny pigs in a pen, he asked for an explanation.

Yi Tongan replied, "We were feeding them barley that had gotten a bit spoiled during this year's rainy season, and they were getting fatter every day. A few days ago, we began to feed them chaff again, but they won't give up their acquired taste for barley, so they lost their appetite. They're getting skinnier every day."

Sotaesan said, "This is a living scripture. The suffering of the rich who become poor, or the powerful, who lose their rank, are no different than the suffering of these pigs. Since time immemorial, all sages have regarded wealth and honor with detachment. They did not become overly happy when wealth and honor came their way nor overly concerned when wealth and honor left. In ancient times, the emperor Shun received the rank of the Son of Heaven after doing such lowly jobs as cultivating the fields and making pottery, but he never became arrogant. Sakyamuni Buddha willingly left his destined position as a king and left the palace, leaving his household life behind. He did not retain even the slightest attachment. How equanimous were their attitudes toward wealth and honor, and how admirable was their power to transcend suffering and happiness.

If you aspire to the Way and want to learn how to be a sage, do not blindly pursue comfort, joy, or power but rather be weary of them. Even if you unavoidably find yourself in such circumstances, do not let yourself become attached or corrupted by them. You will then be able to enjoy eternal comfort, eternal honor, and eternal power."

3

Forgiveness

There was a young man living in a village near Sotaesan who had a spiritual awakening. He recognized his past faults, became Sotaesan's student, and vowed to act as a decent human being. Several months later, Sotaesan returned to Youngsan to find the young man had gone back to his old life. The young man felt ashamed that he had failed to keep his vow, so he avoided Sotaesan.

One day, they happened to meet each other on the road. Sotaesan took the opportunity to ask the young man, "Why is it that you haven't come to see me even once?"

The young man said, "Because I feel guilty."

Sotaesan said, "What do you feel guilty about?"

The young man said, "My vow to you ended up deceiving you. You are a great sage. How could I not feel guilty in front of you? Please forgive me."

Sotaesan replied, "All this time you who have avoided me, squandered all your assets, and placed yourself in compromising situations. You haven't done anything to me and do not need my forgiveness. If your actions were going to harm me, then you would be right to apologize to me or to avoid me. But, in fact, you are the only one who will take the consequences of your actions. Right now, you may think that you deceived me. But in reality, you have deceived yourself. From this point on, do not avoid me, but work hard instead to regulate your own mind, again."

4
———————

Material Civilization and Moral Culture

Sotaesan said, "We live conveniently and profit greatly from the benefits of material civilization and moral culture. Thanks to these benefits, we cannot help but to be grateful to the many inventors and teachers in our world.

However, material civilization mainly provides comforts for our physical lives; its benefits manifest quickly, but its merit is limited. Ethical culture shapes people's minds, which are by nature formless; its benefits are slow, but its merit is unlimited. How can the benefit of cultural ethics' ability to deliver all sentient beings and to cure the world be compared to that of material civilization? How can its radiance be limited to this world alone? It is greatly regrettable that people of our time seek the obvious benefits of material civilization, while very few seek ethical culture."

5
_____

Cause and Effect

Taego asked, "In the Nirvana Sutra it says, 'If we wish to know about our past life, we need to understand that it is what we have received in this present life. If we wish to know about our future life, we need to understand that it is what we create in the present life.' When we observe people receiving blessings or punishments in the present life, we see those who deserve to receive punishments for the way they use their minds but live pleasurable lives as part of rich and distinguished families, while those whose minds are wholesome and who should certainly receive blessings, instead, receive miserable suffering in a poor family. Can we still say that the principle of cause and effect is correct?"

Sotaesan said, "That is why all the buddhas and enlightened masters warn us to hold our final thoughts in a pure and clear fashion. Those whose minds are unwholesome but live a wealthy life in the present are those who, in their past lives, accumulated merit by doing good deeds when they were young, but at the end of their lives fell into unwholesome thoughts by thinking there was no point in performing good. Those whose minds are good but are living a miserable life in the present are those who performed unwholesome deeds unintentionally as youths in their past lives but repented late in their lives and returned to the good. In this way, the final thought in our present life becomes the initial thought in our future life."

6
_____

The So-Called Little Things

Sotaesan always kept his belongings neatly arranged, with everything in its proper place, so that he could find them even in the dark. He kept the temple grounds so well that there was not even a single dust particle out of place.

He said, "If one's personal belongings are messy, one's mind will be messy. Also, if one's temple grounds are dirty, one's mind ground will be untidy as well. If the mind is lazy and unclear, then nothing can be achieved. How can we neglect these so-called little things?"

7

The Essential Discourse on Commanding Our True Nature

1. Believe not in the person alone, but in the dharma.

2. Ponder the dharmas taught by various people and believe in the very best of them.

3. Having been born as humans among all the four forms of birth, we should develop a love of learning.

4. A knowledgeable person should not neglect learning due to a sense of already accomplished knowledge.

5. Do not indulge in wine and sexual misconduct but use the time to inquire into Truth.

6. Do not cling to your biases.

7. When responding to any matter, maintain a respectful state of mind and be vigilant for the rise of covetous greed as if it were a lion.

8. Teach yourself day by day, hour by hour.

9. If things go wrong, do not blame others, but examine yourself.

10. Should you learn of another's fault, do not reveal it but use it instead to perceive your own faults.

8

Best Chanting

A student asked, "Which mantras should I recite, and which method should I apply to open my mind and heart so that I may quickly attain the Way?"

Sotaesan said, "Great practice does not depend on a particular mantra, but rather on a person's sincerity. Let me tell you a couple of stories. Long ago there was an illiterate peddler of straw sandals who was inspired to cultivate the Way. So he asked a sage about the Way. The sage answered, 'mind is buddha' (*chuksim si pul*) but the illiterate peddler thought he heard 'three pairs of straw sandals' (*chipsin se pol*). For many years he recited 'three pairs of straw sandals' and pondered over it, until one day, his mind and heart suddenly opened, and he realized that 'mind is buddha.'

Another practitioner went out to buy some meat and said to the butcher, 'Cut me a piece from the clean part.' The butcher thrust his knife into the meat and asked, 'Which part is clean and which part dirty?'

Upon hearing that question, he attained the Way. These anecdotes clearly show that attaining the Way does not depend on a place, a time, or a mantra. However, since we have our own designated mantras, our merit will increase even more effectively if we resort to them during our dedicated practice."

9

All Water Collects in One Place

While Sotaesan was staying at Pongnae Hermitage, a heavy rain fell, which made a big waterfall descend from a rocky cliff, and all the valley streams flowed vigorously. He watched the sight for a long time, and finally said, "The water flowing down these many valleys is traveling through different courses now, but in the end it will finally collect in a single place. This elucidates the saying 'all dharmas return to one.

10
_____

What is the Most Dispensable?

Sotaesan asked Kim Yongsin, "What is the most indispensable thing for a person living in the secular world?"

Yongsin answered, "I assume things related to clothing, food, and shelter are the most indispensable."

Sotaesan asked, "Which is the most indispensable of the subjects you learned at school?"

Yongsin replied, "The subject of spiritual cultivation was the most indispensable."

Sotaesan answered, "You are right. For the life of the body, clothing, food, and shelter are important things, but for practice, moral cultivation is important. This is why clothing, food, and shelter as well as spiritual cultivation become the foundation for both life and practice. However, the subject of spiritual cultivation that is now taught in schools is insufficient in its methodology. Unless a religion advocates the practice of cultivating the mind, one will not be able to appreciate the full importance of spiritual cultivation. You should constantly bear in mind that the study of the Way is central to all studies and is the foundation of all practice."

11

Skillful Way to Guide

One day Sotaesan visited the Silsang Monastery. He witnessed two elderly monks harshly scolding a young novice who, they said, would not obey their instruction to practice meditation.

They said to the Master, "A person like him could not be delivered even if a thousand buddhas appeared right now. He's useless."

Sotaesan smiled and said, "Though you reverend monks have shown concern for him, you are also preventing him from ever practicing meditation."

One of the senior monks asked, "Why do you say that?"

Sotaesan replied, "By demanding that a person does something he doesn't want to do, you are making him dislike it forever. If I told you that inside the rocks of that mountain there is gold and I demanded that you crack open those rocks and extract the gold, would you trust my words and immediately start mining?"

The elderly monks thought for a while, and said, "It would be hard to believe you and immediately start mining."

Sotaesan said, "In the same way, if I demand that you go mining without first gaining your trust, what would you do? You would most likely think my words are fabricated. When a young student has no interest in meditation or any such aspiration, if you demand that he practice meditation, it will make him presume meditation is also a fabrication. Once he thinks in this way, that would keep him from ever practicing it. Your approach is not a skillful means of guiding a person."

One of the senior monks said, "If this is the case, then what is the skillful means of guiding him?"

Sotaesan said, "Knowing that there is gold inside the rock, if you first go and mine it yourself and then make splendid use of it, people will want to know how you became wealthy. If you tell them the details to suit the degrees of their desire to know, how gratefully they would then go and mine the gold! Wouldn't this be a skillful means of guiding others?"

The senior monks sat up straight and said, "The Master's method of guidance is truly magnificent!"

12

The Sound and Proper Way

One day a student was thatching the roof of a house at the Won Buddhism Headquarters. He laid out the straw but did not tie it down carefully with rope.

Sotaesan said, "If a strong wind blows in the middle of the night, won't all the work you did be for nothing?"

But the student replied, "The wind in this area is rarely so severe," and left the roof as it was.

That night a strong wind arose unexpectedly and blew away the newly thatched roof. The disciple was mortified and distressed. He said, "Great Master, you foresaw with your supernatural powers what would occur and warned me about it. But in my folly, I refused to listen and now I have met with this disaster."

Sotaesan said, "You didn't listen to me when I instructed you in a sound and proper way, but it is even worse that you now call me a psychic. If you think of me in that way, you will not learn the dharma of the great Way from me but will only be on the lookout for psychic powers. This will only put you on a road to nowhere. You must correct your thinking. From now on do everything the sound and proper way.

13

Who Can Learn Completely?

Sotaesan said, "Though the spring breeze blows impartially without discrimination, only living trees can receive its energy and grow. Likewise, sages teach the dharma impartially without any thought of self, yet only those people with belief are ready to receive the dharma completely."

14
_____

Everything is of Our Mind's Creation

Sotaesan came to a meditation session and said, "Yi Inuihwa has now achieved such great clarity of the mind that she neglects her personal business in order to attend dharma meetings and join meditation sessions. Instead of giving her an award for her devoted faith, I would like to allot this hour to her so that she may ask any questions that are on her mind."

Inuihwa asked, "If someone asks me what we teach and learn in our community, how should I reply?"

Sotaesan answered, "Buddhism originally teaches us to awaken and understand the principle, 'all things are created by the mind.' You may answer that we teach and learn the same principle. Once we know it, we will also discover the principle of 'neither arising nor ceasing' and 'the karmic principle of cause and effect.'"

She asked again, "After we learn this principle, how should we practice?"

Sotaesan answered, "We should keep our minds free from disturbances, delusions, and wrong-doings when facing sensory conditions."

15

Timeless Meditation

Zen is a practice that leads to the achievement of freedom of mind through awakening to our own nature, which is originally free from discrimination or attachment. Since time immemorial, those who have been determined to achieve the great Way have all practiced Zen.

If people intend to practice genuine Zen, they first should take true emptiness as the substance and marvelous existence as the function. Externally, be unmoving like Mount Tai when in contact with myriad sensory conditions, and, internally, keep the mind unsullied like empty space. Let the mind function so that it is not active even in action and not resting even at rest. If we do this, then there will be no discrimination that is separate from absorption, so that the functioning of the six sense organs will accord with the original nature of emptiness and calm, numinous awareness. This is what is called Mahayana meditation and it is the method of practice in which we progress in concert through the Threefold Practice.

Therefore, it says in a sutra, "Give rise to a mind that, even while responding, does not dwell anywhere." This is precisely the great dharma of practice that remains unmoved amid myriad sensory conditions. This dharma may seem extremely difficult, but if only we come to understand in detail the methods of its practice, then even a farmer wielding a hoe can practice Zen, as can a carpenter wielding a hammer, a clerk using an abacus, and an official seeing to an administrative matter. However, for people who are first beginning to practice Zen, the mind is not easily controlled according to their wishes. It is like training an ox.

If the reins of the mind are dropped even for a moment, it will instantly harm one's commitment to the Way. Therefore, if you keep exerting yourself without letting go of that spirit which is ready to fight to the bitter end no matter how alluring the sensory conditions may be, the mind gradually will become tamed, and you will reach a state where the mind will do what you wish. Each and every time you are in contact with a sensory condition, do not forget to keep the thought in mind that an opportunity for practice has arrived, always assessing whether or not you are affected by that sensory condition.

Once there is a gradual increase in instances of behavior in which the mind does what you wish, you may from time to time let yourself be put in situations that you normally would find extremely attractive or abhorrent. If the mind is moved as before, then your commitment to the Way is immature; but if it is unmoved, then you will know that this is proof that your commitment to the Way is ripening. However, at the very time that you realize that the mind is unmoving, do not let down your guard, for it is unmoving only through your employing the mental powers, rather than naturally unmoving. The mind will be well tamed only when it remains unmoved when left unguarded.

If you continue for a long time to practice Zen, put an end to all the defilements and achieve freedom of mind, you become centered like an iron pillar and defended from the outside like a stone wall; neither wealth nor status, nor honor or glory, can coax the mind. No one can make your mind submit through the use of weapons or authority. You will never be impeded or obstructed in the practice of any of the dharmas. While residing in this dusty world, you will consistently attain hundreds and thousands of samadhis.

Once you reach this stage, the entire world will be transformed into the one ultimate realm of reality, and right and wrong, good and evil, and all the defiled and pure dharmas will become like the single taste of ghee. This state is called the gateway of nonduality. Freedom from birth and death, liberation from the cycle of rebirths, and the ultimate bliss of the pure land all emerge through this gateway.

Recently groups that practice Zen think that Zen is extremely difficult. There are many who hold that it is impossible to do for someone who has a family or who pursues an occupation, and that you can only practice Zen by entering into the mountains and sitting quietly. This view derives from ignorance of the great dharma, in which all dharmas are nondual. If one can only practice Zen while sitting but not while standing—this would be a sickly Zen, indeed. How could this become the great dharma that can deliver all sentient beings? Moreover, our original nature is not merely limited to emptiness and calmness alone. If we practice Zen like a lifeless log, we would not be practicing the Zen that disciplines our true nature, but instead we would make ourselves into an unstable and helpless person. Therefore, even when involved in a disturbing situation, the mind should be undisturbed. Even when involved in greed-creating sensory conditions, the mind should be unmoving—this is true Zen and true meditation.

To reiterate the main principle of timeless Zen:

"When the six sense organs are free from activity, remove distracted thoughts and nurture the One Mind. When the six sense organs are involved in activity, remove the wrong and nurture the right."

16

Do I Eat too Fast or Talk too Much?

Sotaesan said to a student who ate too fast and talked too much, "Eating a meal or speaking a single word is also practice. If one eats too fast or too much, one is likely to become ill. If one says things that are unnecessary or that deviate from the right Way, then misfortune will occur. Can we, then, be mindless when eating a meal or when speaking a word, even if it is a trivial matter?

A practitioner must see every situation as an opportunity to practice and take pleasure in always responding appropriately. You must set your heart upon this practice."

17

The Value of Dedication

A laywoman asked Sotaesan, "I would like to perform purification rituals and offer prayers like ministers do, but I must work and take care of my family, so I do not have the time or freedom to accomplish this. What should I do?"

Sotaesan said, "Purifying one's mind is no different for either the ordained or the householder. Just purify your own mind and sincerely offer your prayers. Then, there will be absolutely no difference in its efficacy—it will depend only on the degree of your dedication."

18

Seeing the Past and the Future

W hile Sotaesan was staying at Pongnae Hermitage, the wretched shriek of a wild boar that was shot by a hunter, was so pitiful that it prompted him to say, "One's gain is another's loss."

He also said, "Witnessing the death of this wild boar, I can surmise its past deeds; and witnessing this hunter killing the wild boar today, I can also surmise what the hunter will face in the future."

19
_____

How Much Do You Miss Me?

Sotaesan asked the students, "When you have not seen me for a long time, how much do you miss me?" The students replied, "Intensely!"

Sotaesan said, "Undoubtedly so. But understand that no matter how filial children are to their parents, it is hard to compare that to the parents' concern for their children. Likewise, no matter how devoted students are to their teacher, it is hard to compare that to the teacher's concern for them. If a disciple's belief and yearning for their teacher is half as much as the teacher's love and concern for them, then the dharma will definitely be transmitted."

20

The Cost of Receiving Offerings

Sotaesan said, "There was once a meditation master who had many students and lay supporters making sure that his life was comfortable. Even so, he planted several fruit trees and tended them himself to support one of his students with the profit he made from them. The rest of the students asked him why, and the meditation master replied, 'This fellow did not make any merit in his past life, nor is he likely to offer benefits to others in the present life. Supporting him with the grain and money that people donate to make merit would cause him to accumulate even more debts. What he should get is free support in this one lifetime, but when the time comes for him to repay, he would have to go through much suffering as an ox or a horse over many lifetimes. Out of affection I support him in my leisure time to lessen his debt."

The meditation master's handling of this matter is a great dharma instruction for those who live a communal life. You should not dismiss this anecdote lightly! If, with your spirit, body, or material goods, you devote yourself in equal measure for others' sakes, then there would be no harm in accepting people's offerings. However, if you take offerings from people while handling just your own affairs, then you are a person who will incur great debts and must expect to go through much hard work over many lifetimes. Generally, however, those who care for other people do not like to receive others' offerings, but those who are concerned only with their own affairs, do like to receive others' offerings. You must examine yourselves every moment and be cautious not to become a person who incurs great debts from people."

21
<hr />

Listening to a Teacher's

Recommendation

In 1925, after Iksan Won Buddhism Headquarters was first established, the members invested in a taffy-making enterprise in the attempt to sustain their community. Sotaesan always advised his various students, "In today's world, people's minds are not well trained, so be sure to lock the front gate and guard your possessions so nothing gets stolen. If we are robbed, not only do we lose our possessions, but we are also letting others commit transgressions. We must be careful." He then provided them with a lock.

However, due to their inexperience, the students weren't careful in taking precautions, and one night all their taffy molds and candy were stolen. The students could not get over their feelings of shame and anxiety.

Sotaesan said, "Don't worry! The thief who visited us last night was a great teacher for you. You may have believed I was the most respected teacher, yet my warning was not enough to keep you alert. From now on, even if I say nothing, you will be extra careful. Consider the few things you lost last night as the tuition you paid to the teacher."

22

What are We Learning?

Sotaesan asked his students the following question, "If someone were to ask you what you are learning here, what would you answer?"

One of the students said, "I would answer that we are learning the 'three great powers.'"

Another student said, "I would answer that we are learning the 'essential Way of human life.'"

After hearing conflicting answers from several other people, Sotaesan said, "Although all your answers are applicable, I will elaborate a bit, so you must listen carefully! As a rule, whatever answer one gives should be appropriate to the questioner's character and attitude at that time, but to answer in general terms, I would say that I am teaching how to use our mind. To answer more specifically, I teach the knowledgeable how to use knowledge; the powerful how to use power; the wealthy how to use wealth; the resentful how to live a life of gratitude; those who lack merit how to make merit; those who live a life dependent on others to rely on self-power; the reluctant to learn how to learn, those reluctant to teach how to teach, those lacking the desire to benefit others how to dedicate themselves for the benefit of all. In brief, I teach others how to make the most of all their talents, material wealth, and surroundings, in accordance with the right Way."

23

One Pointed Mind

Yang Tosin asked Sotaesan, "We have been trying our best to follow your instructions not to be distracted by one thing while doing another and to always maintain a peaceful and undivided state of mind whatever we're doing. But recently while sewing I also had to prepare an herbal medicine, and I ended up burning the medicine because I was fully engrossed in my sewing. If I were to attend closely to the medicine while I was sewing, that would mean that something distracted me while I was doing something else. On the other hand, if I were to pay close attention only to my sewing and ignore the medicine, I would have to throw out the medicine again. In such a situation, what would be the correct path of practice?"

Sotaesan replied, "If at that time you had to attend to both preparing the medicine and sewing, then both of these duties were your responsibility, and you should have performed them with all sincerity and dedication. Fulfilling well that responsibility reflects a perfect one-pointed mind and true practice. But if you say that you were focusing only on one of those duties, that would not be perfect one pointedness but would be a fragmented and negligent state of mind. Even if you are attending to ten or twenty duties at once, as long as you deal with them with full responsibility, it will not be distraction but an undivided state of mind, and an essential method of practice in action. But, if you are idly thinking about things that are not your concern, idly trying to hear and see things that are not your concern, meddling in things that are not your concern, and thinking of one thing while doing another, and are thereby unable to bring an end to endless wandering thoughts, that is something that practitioners should scrupulously avoid. To pay attention to various things with full responsibility will bring no hindrance at all to your training in one pointed mind, even if you take care of thousands of tasks a day."

24

Freezing Laundry

Whenever Sotaesan visited Seoul, he stayed at the Seoul Won Buddhist temple. Yi Kongju usually attended to his needs and listened to his dharma talks. Cho Chongwon would prepare the meals and clean, so she rarely had a chance to listen to the talks. She would constantly think about ways to listen to the Master. Even when she was cooking in the kitchen, she would sometimes take the firewood out of the fireplace and listen to him speaking. She could not enter the room where Sotaesan was, because she feared she smelled from all the cooking, and that she might burn the food if she got distracted. So she had to be satisfied with eavesdropping.

Sometimes, when others were studying in a warm room, Cho Chongwon had to stay outside and do laundry in the freezing water. During the winter solstice, she ate some red-bean porridge and was on her way to do the laundry when it started to snow. Her hands felt so frozen that she repeatedly blew on them, tucked them under her arms, and took them out again to wash the clothes. By the time she was finished, her hands felt like they were about to break. She was walking back with tears in her eyes, when Sotaesan opened the door and exclaimed, "I can feel the cold inside this room. It must be freezing outside!"

Sotaesan quickly took the basket of laundry from her. He followed her to the kitchen, took her cold hands in his warm hands and said, "Even if you had committed many transgressions throughout many lifetimes, by doing this work now for the good of the many, you have lightened that burden. Let your conscience be clear and your mind unhindered."

Cho Chongwon cried at his comforting words.

Later, whenever she faced challenges and felt overwhelmed, she thought back to that moment and said to herself, "I am paying back the many misdeeds of my previous life," and thus consoled herself.

Part 2

OPENING THE EYE OF WISDOM

25

The Farmer Who Ran to the Reservoir

Sotaesan talked about directing our thoughts wards the benefit of others. "Once upon a time, it rained so hard that all the townspeople ran out to their fields with shovels. One person, however, left his field behind and ran toward the reservoir, knowing that saving his one field from flooding would not save the rest of the fields from being ruined if the reservoir failed. That person's eagerness for the benefit of all saved them."

26

Other People's Money

When Sotaesan was buying land in Youngsan, it took him a month to bargain for the lowest price. Yi Wanchol asked Sotaesan, "How can a person of virtue like you haggle over money?"

He responded, "This money came from people's donations. Every penny belongs to the people. Public money should be spent very carefully. It is a great transgression to be wasteful with public money."

27
_____

A Buddha Offering

Once, while Sotaesan was residing at Pongnae Hermitage, an old couple passing by commented that they were on their way to Silsang Monastery to make a buddha offering. Their daughter-in-law, they explained, was very ill-tempered and disrespectful. Upon hearing their problem, Sotaesan said to them, "How is it that you know to make a buddha offering to the buddha image but not to the living buddha?"

The old couple asked, "Where is the living buddha?"

Sotaesan replied, "The daughter-in-law who lives in your home is the living buddha. Since she is the one with the ability to be either respectful or disrespectful, why don't you try making an offering to her first?"

"How should we make such an offering?"

"With the money you were going to use for the buddha offering, buy her a gift she would appreciate and treat her with the same respect you would the buddha. Then, depending on how sincere you are, the effect of your buddha offering will manifest."

When the couple returned home, they did as they were told and ultimately, in a few months, the daughter-in-law indeed became loving and filial. The old couple returned to Sotaesan and thanked him over and over again. Sotaesan said to his students sitting beside him, "This is a practical buddha offering; one that goes directly to the source of transgressions and merits."

28
_____

What Kind of a Person?

A student asked, "What kind of person receives the most blessings in the next life?"

Sotaesan replied, "A person who dedicates himself to the wellbeing of others through his body, spirit, and material."

"Then what kind of person receives the most suffering in the next life?"

"A person who has only taken from others through body, spirit, and material."

"What kind of person is most at peace?"

"A person who knows his place and can be at peace no matter what happens."

"What kind of person is the wealthiest and has the most treasure?"

Sotaesan replied, "A person who can be thankful for what they have and is satisfied in all situations."

29
_____

How to Change Our very Essence

Sotaesan told his students, "If you cut off a limb of a lotus-persimmon tree and graft a persimmon tree onto it, you get regular persimmon despite the roots being lotus-persimmon. If you cut off a thornbush at the stump and graft a rosebush onto it, roses will grow. Much like the persimmon and rosebush, you must perform mind practice by cutting off the poisonous mind, while grafting on a buddha mind. Do not let any distraction come between your intention and your practice.

This is like a caterpillar turning into a butterfly or larvae turning into a cicada which sings through the night. When a fly is just a maggot, it is very limited. But when it becomes a fly, it can live in the king's chambers, eat the king's food and sleep in the king's bed. We must change in the same way. We must study how to change our very essence."

30

Tidying Our Minds

Sotaesan taught us that even while tidying our things, we must always maintain the practicing mind. "I tell you to clean properly in the hope that you will also sweep away your distracting thoughts. Essentially, our mind is pure. However sometimes, depending on the situation, that pure mind can be poisoned with jealousy, greed and hate. Just as we clean the house that we live in, we should clean our minds. We must get rid of the root of our distractions, just like pulling out weeds. Tidying your things is a way to tidy your mind. When your mind is distracted, it reflects on your surroundings. If your belongings are in disarray, that means your mind is just as unstable. Even if you have pulled out most of the weeds, if you do not finish the job, there is no point in cleaning.

Likewise, even if you get rid of all your distractions, if you do not practice organizing the mind, there is no point in mind practice. Therefore, always maintain the habit of organizing your belongings and your home, so that it may reflect on your mind practice."

31

Your Purpose

When the children living at the Won Buddhism Headquarters came to say good morning to Sotaesan, he would think well of them and give them some snacks.

One time during an evening class, he said, "At first, I commended these children for stopping by every morning and saying hello. But now, I do not know if their purpose is to say good morning or to receive snacks from me. Ask yourself, what is your purpose for being in this place? We must always think of the reasons and purposes behind everything. No matter what hardships you face, you must not forget the original purpose that you had."

32

The Value of a Single Grain of Rice

A student was washing some rice and dropped some on the floor. Sotaesan picked up a single grain and told the other students to do the same. He said, "If we are reckless with this grain that the farmers worked so hard for, we will receive the retribution of being without food in the future. We must know the value of each grain and be grateful."

33
_____

To Spit toward the Sky

Sotaesan said, "A bad person harming a good person is like spitting towards the sky. You're only spitting towards yourself because it falls down. It is also like sweeping dirt towards the wind. The dirt is brought back to you. Harming a good person will eventually lead to harming yourself."

34

The Difficult Path or the Easy Path

Sotaesan and his student, Yi Chunpung, were climbing a steep mountain behind Chongnyon Hermitage.

Sotaesan said, "Climbing a steep pass naturally enhances my one-pointed mind practice. You rarely stumble on a steep trail but are actually more prone to stumble on a level trail. We are more prone to make mistakes with an easy task than a difficult one. A practitioner who maintains consistency on either steep or level trails, or on easy or difficult tasks, will achieve single minded concentration."

35

How to Own a Train

Aperson visited Sotaesan and during their conversation he said, "The train between Jeonju and Iksan is run by the wealthy people of this Jeolla region, and they are allowed to ride the train for free." In saying this the visitor showed his envy.

Sotaesan said, "Have you not made that train yours yet? You must be very poor."

The man was very surprised and asked, "I would imagine it takes a huge amount of money to own a train. How can a poor man like me do that?"

Sotaesan replied, "Even if you owned your own train, I would not call you wealthy. I already own not just that train, but all the trains in the world. I have done so for a long time now. Have you not heard?"

The man became even more shocked and said, "I have not heard anything like that. I am afraid I am not capable of understanding what you mean."

Sotaesan said, "If a person is to own a train, he has to spend a fortune and be tormented with the upkeep. But the way I own it does not take a huge amount of money, nor do I need to take responsibility for the train. Whenever I desire to go somewhere, I simply pay a certain amount and then use the train however I please. On a similar note, a while ago, I went to Seoul and visited the park. I was enjoying the fresh air and all the benefits of that park but no one told us to leave or never to come again.

Owning a small garden at a resort would cost a fortune, but I could enjoy that park just as much without any payment. The desire to own something is simply for one's own personal comfort. However, I use the train and the park as much as I want—how is that not better? This is why I say I own them all. Everything in this world—the earth, the mountains—are all mine. I use them when I need to, as long as I follow basic manners and rules. No one can tell me to do otherwise. My household is therefore, very large. However, most people have such a small mind, that they only concentrate on owning whatever they can. Then they worry about all the work and the responsibility that follows, which is why they cannot see the bigger picture."

36
_____

Learning to Adapt

Sotaesan said, "You must learn to adapt. A stubborn person will encounter many obstacles. For example, you must put away your thick winter clothes and change into lighter clothes when spring comes. The same goes for your job. If you feel like you cannot live on your salary, you must consider your situation and your skills, and decide if it is better to run your own business or turn to farming. If you are stubborn enough to say that you cannot change your job, then you will fall into debt, lose your credit, and possibly ruin your household.

Meditation practice is no different. If you have entered a meditation session, then you must come to the hall as soon as the practice bell rings and focus on your mind practice. But if a situation happens—such as your parents' deaths, or an illness in your family—you must halt and go home. If you insist that you cannot stop your mind practice and fail to do your duties as a human being, that is obstinacy."

37
_____

The Truth Does not Have Form

Sotaesan said, "The truth is not in books, it is in the universe. For example, if you study the sun at daytime, it seems like it will be bright forever—but it moves west in a few hours and disappears. Then it reappears on the east side the next morning. Studying the teachings of the sages is to wonder, 'Where does the sun go?' And by studying, you will learn the truth that night embraces day just as day embraces night. The two are not separate. Then you have reached the truth.

Also, during the four seasons, the cold season comes from the warm season as the warm season comes from the cold season. Our pain and happiness, wealth and poverty, are linked like a head to a tail. They are created by our six sense organs. Receiving high praise because of your bachelor's degree or doctorate degree, derives from the fact that you went through much hardship as a student. Your wealth allows you to eat and dress well. This also derives from the fact that you worked very hard to make money. On the other hand, some people become completely broke after being rich, and some people suffer by losing their beloved children. If we seek to find the cause, we will know that they had transgressed in the past.

Therefore, the myriad phenomena in the universe, and all things with or without form, are connected. Happiness and pain, being wealthy and being poor—all the changes among them are the formless scripture that teaches us the truth of the buddhadharma."

38
_____

Skipping Morning Mediation

Cheon Gooil was in charge of ringing the bell at the Won Buddhism Headquarters. He was to strike the bell for morning meditation at 5 am every morning. One time, he misread the clock and rang the bell at 1 am. The people at the Headquarters heard the bell and gathered at the Great Enlightenment Hall to participate in morning meditation. When they realized it was only one o'clock, they started to argue about whether or not they should do the meditation.

"The bell rang; we have no choice. We should start meditating right now."

"But there is still four hours left for the sun to rise. How are we supposed to meditate until then? We should go back and wake up again at five."

"We are all tired from lack of sleep right now. How can we wake up at five? We should meditate right now, go back to sleep until the sun rises, and not ring the bell at five."

After a heated discussion, they reached the conclusion that they could not meditate for four hours, nor could they wake up again at five. So they went back to their beds to sleep through the sunrise. Upon hearing this, Sotaesan became angry.

"Just because you woke up at a mistaken time, does not make it right to sleep right until morning! That conclusion is ridiculous! How can you wish to become buddha one day with that attitude? The mind practice should keep you busy, as if your beard is on fire! A practitioner of the Way should never miss his meditation even if he has to miss a meal.

You have all come here to study and practice, but instead, you break the rules and skip meditation—you are worse today than you were yesterday, and can never in this way do anything for the common good. What happened this morning was your mistake, so you must all reflect upon what you did wrong and work so that it never happens again."

39

The Reason Behind Great Talent

When Taeho, Kim Jungmook's brother, was seven years old, he went to the Won Buddhist temple with his friends. When he saw the portrait of Buddha on the altar, he said, "Even I can draw that." Hearing this, a priest brought him some paper and a brush. Taeho took the brush, dipped it in paint and began painting a portrait exactly like the one at the temple. Everyone was so amazed that they sent the piece to the administrative office, and the teachers in the area all came and gasped at his talent. They even had a wager on him. Eventually, the teachers said that a genius like this had to be trained, and with their teachings, Taeho's skills grew every day. He would forget about the time of day or even the seasons of the year and focused on painting.

Seeing his talent and hard work, everyone said that he would grow up to be a famous artist. His skills eventually reached a limit, and then would not grow any further. No matter how hard he worked, he could not improve. So his brother, Kim Jungmook, asked Sotaesan the reason. The Master replied, "Have you ever cultivated land?" "Yes, I have."

"A land that has been cultivated before is easier the second time. Your brother's case is no different. The reason he could draw the portrait with such ease at first was that he had great artistic talents in his previous life. However, now that his skills have reached the capacity of his previous life, it is just like cultivating new land. It is difficult and slow. If he wishes to become a great artist, he has to keep on trying.

Thomas Edison made many inventions, but that did not happen in his one short lifetime. He had practiced his talent and skill throughout many lifetimes, and that hard work had eventually paid off in the lifetime when he was born in the 19th century.

Another man by the name of Huineng, the Sixth Patriarch of Chinese Zen Buddhism was a woodcutter, who became greatly enlightened and attained buddhahood when he heard the phrase, 'Give rise to a mind that does not dwell anywhere.' This was possible because he was a great holy man in his previous life."

Part 3

WHERE IS THE AWAKENED ONE?

40

Shiny Radishes

During the winter retreat, everyone would share the food that the members brought after evening studies. One day, Tak Boshingap, who was a young bride, participated in the evening studies. She wanted to bring something delicious for Sotaesan and her companions. But her house was so poor, she could not find even a single thing to bring.

One day, while searching her storeroom, she noticed a small vegetable garden growing out of the dirt floor. She remembered burying a few radishes there, and excitedly pulled them out. She carefully washed and dried them with great care. She polished them so well that they began to shine. That night, she wrapped the radishes in a bundle and took them to the temple.

After the study session was over, the members took out dried persimmons, sweet rice cake treats and all sorts of tasty snacks for Sotaesan. Seeing this, Boshingap became embarrassed and could not offer the radishes. Then, Sotaesan said, "Boshingap, what have you brought?" Boshingap, who had become red with embarrassment, could not lift her head as she took out her bundle for Sotaesan. "Go on, open it." he urged her. Reluctantly, she opened the bundle and revealed the shiny, white radishes.

Sotaesan said, "Let's all share these radishes that Boshingap has brought to the community." He ate a radish on the spot and declared out loud how delicious it was. Her embarrassment disappeared and a smile filled her face.

41
_____

Aengdu's Father, the Buddha

Aengdu's father worked at the Won Buddhism Headquarters, mainly cleaning toilets and performing other odd tasks. Even in the middle of his unpleasant labor, Aengdu's father would always stop by when Sotaesan was giving a lecture to his students. There, he would sit on the wooden porch outside and listen.

One summer day, Sotaesan was engaged in teaching when there was a foul smell coming from the toilet. Everyone started whispering and looked outside to find Aengdu's father listening outside on the porch. He had been cleaning the toilet and had temporarily left his carrier full of excrement outside. Everyone frowned and pinched their noses.

Seeing this, Sotaesan scolded them all. "You are all foolish. Where do you think buddha is? That man is a buddha and the filth he carries is a buddha. You all sit here in your beautiful clothes and listen to good words; do you think that makes you a better person? If you are not grateful to the person who does something for you, you are wrong. If you are displeased with the person who does dirty work for a living, thinking he smells and wanting him to leave, then you are wrong. How are you better than that man? If you belittle him just because of his job, then you are wrong."

42

Seeing Only the Faults in People

One student had a narrow mind—he only saw what was bad in people. Sotaesan heard his story and told him, "What sort of eyes do you have? Why do you only see and speak of what is bad in people? From now on, strive to see and speak of the good in people. In that way, others can see the good in you too."

43

_____

The Orangutan and the Alcohol

Sotaesan said, "In many cases, huge transgressions start with small mistakes. You should constantly observe your own behavior and correct even minor errors. There is an animal in Asia called the orangutan, known to be so exceptionally strong and fast that it cannot be caught by man. But this animal enjoys alcohol. So, if you leave out a jar of liquor in the middle of the road, the orangutan will see it when it passes by. At first, it will smile and be on its way; then it will return to take a sip and go on again. But it will return again to take another sip. After repeating this several times, the liquor will be gone, and the animal will become so intoxicated that it will collapse. Then a person can come and easily capture it. A sip became a whole jar, and ultimately led to the animal's capture and demise.

A person is no different. A person cannot correct his small mistakes at first. These mistakes continue to grow and grow into a larger problem. So, you should all be alert to your own small mistakes."

44

The Honest Child

Sotaesan had stayed in Seoul for a long time. When he came back to the Won Buddhism Headquarters, all of his students gathered to greet him. He looked around and asked the children, "Did you miss me?"

Kilju and Dongho replied, "We did!"

Sotaesan asked the same question to Pallo, who was silent. "How about you?" "Not really," Pallo answered.

The Master laughed out loud at this and said, "You are right. Why would a young man like you miss me?" Sotaesan praised Pallo for being so honest.

45

Confess Your Faults Beforehand

One day, Sotaesan took some herbal medicine for his rash. Chong Sewol, who was in charge of the kitchen asked, "Who would like to boil down his medicine?"

Kim Jihyun said she would do it.

So she started to boil the medicine, but she waited too long and it burned. Panicked, she poured some water on the medicine and brought it to Sotaesan. He said, "You burned this, right?"

She replied in a tiny voice, "Yes."

Sotaesan said, "Then you should have told me. When you confess your faults beforehand, you decrease them.'

46
_____

Changing Fate

Sotaesan told a story:

During the Tang Dynasty in China, there was a famous prime minister named Baehyu. He was born with his twin brother, conjoined at his back. Their parents separated them with a knife and named the bigger child "Baedo" calling him the older one. They named the smaller child "Baetak"and called him the younger one. "Baehyu" is the name that Baedo went by once he reached adulthood.

The brothers became orphaned at a young age, so they lived with their uncle. One day, a well-known Buddhist priest came by the house, and looked at the boys closely. He requested to talk to their uncle, and asked him, "Who are those two boys?"

"They are my family. I have raised them since their parents' early deaths."

"You have to make them leave."

"Why?" the uncle asked.

"I have seen their future and they both have a destiny to become beggars. They have no good fortune whatsoever, so if you keep them, not only will your house become poor, but your neighbors will become poor as well. For those boys to follow their destiny as beggars, they will bankrupt your household. Let them go before they ruin your life."

Baedo overheard this conversation, and after the priest left, he confronted his uncle, "Uncle, my brother and I want to leave. Please give us your blessing."

The Uncle was astonished, "Leave? What do you mean?"

"I overheard what the priest told you earlier. If my brother and I are destined to be poor and damned, how can we bring your household down with us? We will leave. Please give us your blessing."

The uncle protested, but the brothers left and became beggars, scrounging every day for food.

One day, after discussing their situation they said, "If we keep living like this, our parents will not be able to rest in peace. Let's go into the mountains. We can sell charcoal, study, and learn martial arts."

So the brothers went into the mountains and sold charcoal. They studied many books and practiced with their swords. They made more than enough charcoal to get by. They bundled up the remainder with handwritten letters and placed them on doorsteps. "We made this charcoal with heart and sincerity. Please do not feel burdened, feel free to use it."

Days, months, and years passed. The brothers continued to leave the charcoal for their neighbors. The people who received these presents were suspicious at first, but soon became grateful. They even left bowls of rice outside their doors for the brothers to take. But the brothers never took more than they needed. "This will be plenty, thank you." The news about these brothers soon spread, reaching their uncle. He went to them, and pleaded with them, "Please, come home with me, even for a short while." When they got to the house, the priest was there again. The priest, after looking at Baedo, expressed his shock. "You now have the face of a man who will be an asset to his country."

Baedo responded, "You used to tell us that we had the fortune of beggars. Why do you say something so different today?"

"Your face had a beggar's fortune in the past, but now it does not. What have you done over the years?" When the brothers told him in detail, the priest happily remarked, "Of course! Your good heart has changed your future."

As the priest predicted, Baedo went on to become the prime minister of his country, using the name Baehyu. Baetak was offered a government position but refused. Instead, he worked as a boatman on the Hwangha River, and lived a plain but noble life.

Sotaesan finished his story and said, "You should not go to fortune tellers. Through mind practice you are changing your present and your future. If you follow my teachings well, you do not need to have your fortune told."

47

Always Keep a Promise

One day, Sotaesan and a few of his students were walking out of the Won Buddhism Headquarters. Children who were playing outside bowed to him, except for the youngest child. Sotaesan stroked the child's head and said, "If you bow, I will give you a snack." At his words, the child bowed.

The adults kept walking and were laughing at what had just happened, but Sotaesan stopped in his tracks. "Wait here. I must do something."

He went back into his room and soon came out with a snack. He gave it to the child, and then continued on his way with his disciples.

Sotaesan always kept his promise, no matter how small.

48

On Predators and Poisonous Snakes

Astudent asked Sotaesan, "If animals and trees are buddhas, then are those who harm humans, such as predators and poisonous snakes, buddhas too?"

Sotaesan replied, "If predators and poisonous snakes harm you, do not fight them. Respect the buddha by stepping aside and avoiding conflict."

The student asked again, "Then are insects and bacteria buddhas too?"

Sotaesan replied, "It is certain that they are! So do not kill them recklessly. The reason they sometimes harm you is to protect themselves so that they can continue to live."

49

Live in Happiness and Satisfaction

Yi Tongan asked Sotaesan, "What must you do to deliver sentient beings?"

Sotaesan said, "You must bring happiness to those in pain, teach those who do not know about the truth, and draw the good out of those who are not. In order to deliver liberation to others, you must live in happiness and satisfaction, be bright and wise, and pour your heart and mind into everything you do."

50

A Teacher's True Intentions

When one of his students did something wrong, Sotaesan would scold them in front of all the others. However, he always worried that the rest of them would dislike the student. So he told them, "You may dislike the transgression, but do not dislike the person. I may have scolded him, but the rest of you should go and console him. Stop him if he tries to leave and go comfort him."

In that way Sotaesan always took care of his students and never left a student behind.

51

Begging For a Blessing

A beggar came to Sotaesan's student, Kim Kichon, and asked for money, saying that doing so would bless him. Kim Kichon asked, "If I am generous with you, how will you give me a blessing?" The beggar could not answer him. Kichon said, "Foolish men tell people to be charitable for their own personal good. That is far from a blessing; it is a misdeed."

Sotaesan heard this, and said, "Kichon's words are very true. People in this world love to receive blessings but most dislike to give them. People dislike to be the receiver of misdeeds, but many commit them. That is why this world is filled with people who are suffering, and so few are happy."

52

The Father Respects the Son

When he was on his deathbed, Sotaesan spoke to Song Pyokcho, "You are a Confucian scholar. If a son has a higher position than his father in the government, how should the father treat the son?"

"He treats his son with appropriate respect. Even if they are biologically father and son, he must still be respectful."

This was Sotaesan's way of telling Song Pyokcho to follow and respect his son Song Gyu, who later became the Second Head Dharma Master of Won Buddhism after Sotaesan's passing.

53

Dedication to the Master

When Sotaesan was near his death, he often called upon his old students who had worked hard with him to build the community.

One day, he called to the kitchen, "Prepare a table for Tohwa next to mine." Choe Tohwa refused and insisted she would eat on the floor.

"I cannot eat with you," she said.

"Ever since you met me, you have not eaten a meal in comfort, nor have you lived in luxury. You have been through many hardships just because you met me."

She cried in response to the warmth in his words. He continued, "I have to go to the Diamond Mountains to cultivate my mind. Can you do well without me?"

"If you go, I will go too."

"I am going somewhere you cannot come."

"That is not possible. I will follow you anywhere."

"You will follow me? That would not be easy. You will know when I disappear."

54

The Student who Buried a Dead Body

I t was summer, the last night of the lunar month. Sotaesan told Kim Hyongoh, "Did you notice the corpse lying by the mulberry trees? Go take care of it."

The place had no houses, and was known to be visited frequently by thieves, so Kim Hyongoh felt reluctant. "What are you thinking? Once the body loses the spirit, it is no different from a dead fish. So go ahead."

"I will." she said.

Kim Hyongoh was on her way, but she became too afraid. So she went to Kim Ilhyun's house and called out, "Ilhyun, are you there?" From inside the house she heard, "Who is it?"

"It's me. Did you know there is a dead body by the mulberry trees?"

"What? Are you sure?"

"Master Sotaesan told me to take you along to take care of it. Come with me."

"Is that really true?"

"Would I misrepresent Sotaesan and lie to you?"

"Alright, I'll go."

They took a lamp and a wheelbarrow and went over to the mulberry trees. There was a dead body wrapped in a straw mat. Together they dragged the body over to the wheelbarrow and then buried it nearby. It was around eleven o'clock when they were done. Sotaesan was waiting for them. He had not gone to bed. Kim Hyongoh said, "I was too afraid to go alone, so I lied and brought Ilhyun with me. We buried the body with much care."

"Although you lied, you did do as I asked," said Sotaesan. "Isn't it good to take care of an ownerless corpse? It is our duty to set an example by doing things most people want to avoid."

55

Karmic Principle

Cho Chongwon asked Sotaesan, "Since for many lifetimes the buddhas have done nothing to receive lowly retributions, there should be no occasion for them to experience suffering in their numerous lifetimes. However, in the past the Buddha has endured various hardships. You too, Great Master, after establishing this community, have not been spared the suffering from government surveillance as well as troubles dealing with the congregation. We do not understand the reason for this."

Sotaesan replied, "Even though I have been delivering many people throughout several lifetimes, and although it has already been quite some time since I have committed any transgression knowingly, I unknowingly repressed the unwholesome energies of obstinate beings." He continued, "Even with a buddha's ability, which brings about compassionate deliverance with the right dharma, one cannot eliminate one's fixed karma; No matter how insignificant a sentient being may be, one's merits may not be offset by one's transgressions. Buddhas and bodhisattvas of great ability can, indeed, condense into a single lifetime the retributions they were to receive over many lifetimes, but they can never eliminate them completely."

56

Using the New Hair Clipper

Sotaesan said, "This morning, Kim Sam Maehwa was shaving my head, but the hair clipper didn't work well and kept pulling my hair. So she told me, 'Master, the clipper must be broken.' I had bought that clipper recently at a shop in Seoul, with Lee Kongju, and had picked the best one. So I took the clipper back to the Won Buddhism Headquarters and asked Park Daewan to shave my head. He did it with much ease and took very little time, and said to me, 'It is a good machine.' I asked Jeon Eumgwang as well, and he too told me that the clipper was very good. Then I asked Song Doseong, but he had a difficult time, so I thought his technique was lacking.

Instead of thinking that her skills were deficient, Sam Maehwa blamed the machine. A person who is skilled recognizes that the machine is good and appreciates it. But a person who is unskilled cannot use a good machine, let alone appreciate it. It is the same with people. If you have dealt with many people, you can recognize their strengths and weaknesses, and instruct them accordingly. If we are only able to see the weaknesses, we end up scolding them, instead of getting along and giving them a good purpose. A person who has attained complete realization knows how to work with all types of people, but deluded beings do not know how, and only see flaws in others.

A long time ago, Sakyamuni Buddha even knew how to deal with a person like Jodal, who tried to harm the Buddha. Jodal would go around spreading bad rumors about him. But Buddha said, 'Jodal is a buddha too, no different from me. Actually, he is working even harder than I am. I sit comfortably here in ultimate bliss, telling people to throw away their suffering and come join me. However, Jodal is in hell, actively teaching people not to follow his footsteps. Jodal is saving more people than I am.' Buddha could not have acted as Jodal did, and yet, he knew how to extract wisdom from a person like Jodal. Still, Jodal denied Buddha till the end, and could not avoid hell. So my students, you must study and practice to attain buddhahood."

57

Why Cut off Your Hand?

W hen the Chinese Buddhist monk, Hyega, was studying under Bodhidharma, he cut off his own hand to show his faith. Like Hyega, So Taewon cut his left hand off to show his faith and devotion to Sotaesan. When So Taewon came back from the hospital, Sotaesan asked him, "Taewon, why did you cut off your hand? Because you did not want to work? Because you wanted to rest?"

"No." "Then why?"

"Truthfully, I was thinking about the story of Master Hyega and how he cut off his own hand."

"What? You were trying to copy him?"

"I was not trying to copy him. I thought that in order to achieve enlightenment, I had to have enough faith to cut off my own hand."

"So you were comparing me to Bodhidharma, and yourself to Master Hyega?"

"That is right."

"That is not a very good comparison. I will see if you truly understand the meaning of the story. Go ahead and tell me the story of Bodhidharma and Master Hyega."

So Taewon began his story, "Bodhidharma came from India to China and practiced for nine years at Shaolin Monastery. Then one snowy winter, Master Hyega came to see Bodhidharma to ask for his wisdom. At first, Bodhidharma ignored him, but Hyega did not move until the snow piled up to his knees. And Bodhidharma said he would pass down the great dharma only to those with enough faith to sacrifice their whole body. Upon hearing this, Master Hyega cut off his hand in front of Bodhidharma to show his faith."

Sotaesan replied, "He showed his faith but could not settle his mind, so he asked Bodhidharma, 'My mind is not at peace. Please put my mind to rest.' Then what did Bodhidharma say?"

"He said, 'Show me your disturbed mind, then I will settle it for you.'"

But Master Hyega could not find his unsettled mind anywhere. So what did he ask Bodhidharma?

"He said, 'I cannot find it anywhere.'"

"Then what did Bodhidharma say?"

"He said, 'If you cannot find your disturbed mind, then your mind is already settled.'"

"Then what happened?"

"Master Hyega achieved enlightenment."

"Then did Master Hyega attain enlightenment by cutting off his hand, or did he do so by Bodhidharma's words?"

"It was his words."

"If you know so well, then why did you cut off your hand? To show me your strong faith? What will come of that?"

"Why can't you say anything? You are good with your words."

"Master, I have done wrong."

"Taewon, you have much potential for the future. What if later on, future members of our Order try to emulate you and cut off their hands too? What should we do then?"

So Taewon sat silently.

"Taewon, again I say that you have so much potential. How can someone like you make such a foolish mistake? What if our future members try to follow in your footsteps by cutting off their hands as well? What can we do then?"

So Taewon said nothing.

"Listen, Taewon. Our human body is the most important tool for our practice and work. What's the use of demonstrating your faith if you damage it? True faith comes from the mind, not the body. Our Order is still beginning, so we have many things to do. If you cut off your hand and cannot work, then who will? You must never do anything like this again! No matter how knowledgeable you are, and even if you received much respect from others, or from past actions, that does not make you a true believer. Only a person who is willing to make the utmost effort with unwavering faith can be a true master in this world."

58
_____

The Killing of Insects

Kim Joongmook was working on a peach farm, and he killed many insects with insecticides. He started to think that perhaps by killing seemingly insignificant lives, he was violating a natural law.

So he asked Sotaesan. The Master replied, "Who did you do this work for?"

"I worked for the development of Won Buddhism," Kim Joongmook answered.

Sotaesan said, "Yes, you did. You did not do it for your personal gain. The insects were eating what belonged to the public for their personal growth. Admiral Yi Sunshin killed people, not worms. But we don't say that he committed a transgression. Instead we praise him and say he did the right thing for the common good. A person who works for the common good, progresses. You, too, will progress and become a better person in your next life.

Even so, if you were serving the greater good, you will receive karmic consequences. That is inevitable. But those consequences will not be as severe. For example, killing thousands of bugs may give you a small boil. So do not be afraid of the acts you do for the public good. If you have the slightest inclination to do it for your own personal satisfaction, then the karmic consequences will not be light, so be careful!"

59

Make Your Promise Known

Park Chegwon decided to be a Won Buddhist minister when she graduated from school. She visited Master Sotaesan to tell him of her decision. She was in her second year at one of the best schools in the area, Jeonbuk Girl's High School. Sotaesan told her to tell the public of her determination.

Chegwon thought, "Whether I tell the public or not, it will not affect my decision. I have made a promise to Master Sotaesan. I know I will not break it. There is no need to inform the public of my decision."

Sotaesan said, "You must make your decision known to the many! In that way, you become more responsible to your word. If you keep that decision to yourself, it could go wrong. You may not think so now, but it can change as you grow older. I once knew someone who attended your school and who, like you, said she wished to be a Won Buddhist minister. Later she changed her mind and got married. If you make your decision public, you can ask the people for support, even if you change your mind later. In that way, you are able to keep the original promise that you made."

60

The Darkness beneath the Lamp

W hile Sotaesan was staying at Pongnae Hermitage, he pointed at a lamplight and asked, "Why does that lamplight illuminate all directions except directly underneath?"

Kim Namchon replied, "This is exactly how I am. I have been the Great Master's direct attendant for several years, but what I know and can do is inferior to that of my dharma brothers who come from afar occasionally to visit you."

Sotaesan smiled and asked Song Kyu the same question. Song Kyu replied, "The light of that lamp shines upward illuminating the far distance, but the lamp stand dims everything underneath. If we take this as a simile, this is just like certain people who are well aware of others' faults but are blind to their own mistakes. The reason is that when they look at other people, there is nothing blocking their view, so they can directly look upon the strengths and weaknesses and good or bad points, but when they look at themselves, the shadow of the ego covers the light of wisdom, preventing them from recognizing their own right and wrong conduct."

Sotaesan asked, "What then can an imperfect person do to illuminate everything without bias?"

Song Kyu replied, "If one is not attached to joy, anger, sorrow, or pleasure and eliminates all notions from the mind, then one's understanding will be free from self and others."

Sotaesan said, "You are right."

61

Which Part is Clean and

Which Part is Dirty?

This is a story that Sotaesan told:

There was an unnamed Buddhist priest who was leading a monastic life. One day, his son came and said, "Father, tomorrow is the anniversary of grandfather's death."

"Is that so? Then we must go and prepare the appropriate food for the ceremony."

The priest went to the butcher shop with some money and said, "I need some meat. It will be used in an important ritual, so please try to cut me a clean piece."

The butcher stuck his knife in the meat and asked, "Which part is clean and which part is dirty?"

The priest was baffled, and he said, "You are right. Nothing is either clean or dirty. There are no clean or dirty parts, hateful or lovely parts." The priest had experienced deep enlightenment.

Sotaesan said, "The dharma instructions are not the only ways to attain enlightenment. If you keep studying and practicing, you will eventually come to realize on your own."

62

What Happens to Others
Happens to Me

Mun Chonggyu, one of Sotaesan's students said to the Master, "A while ago, I went to Park Hojang's house and it happened to be the anniversary of his son's death. Seeing him grieve deeply made me realize how profoundly hurt he was."

Sotaesan said, "The bond between a parent and a child is so deep, it is normal to grieve so." The student replied, "I do not understand. He is a practitioner, yet he loses his head over something so meaningless? How does that make sense?"

Sotaesan asked him, "Can you tell me that if something like that happened to you, you would not be upset?"

"I would not be upset at all." "Are you sure?"

Sotaesan asked repeatedly, and the student repeatedly answered the same. A few years later, one of that student's sons had a legal problem, and was locked in prison for twenty days or so. He was so worried that he could not eat or sleep. He would constantly wander around the house, crying. Later, he visited Sotaesan and said, "I realize now that there is a big difference between watching what happens to others, and actually experiencing it myself. I am very sorry to have made a false statement to you back when I mentioned Park Hojang."

Sotaesan said, "You are right. Ordinary people talk big and act foolishly about the things they only observe. Since you have realized what is wrong, you should always keep this in mind."

63

The Student Who Plucked the Pine Leaves

This is the story told by Hwang Chongsinhaeng when she was going to her vacation home in Yangju with Sotaesan. One day Sotaesan said to her, "I hear you own some good land. Can I take a look?"

Chongsinhaeng said, "If you wish to look, I can guide you."

The next day, Chongsinhaeng packed a snack and went with four people, including Yi Wanchol. While they were walking, Chongsinhaeng, with no reason, began plucking pine needles from the trees. Sotaesan asked, "Why are you picking pine needles?"

Yi Wanchol next to her said, "Sometimes we cannot help but to break a few branches when we hike in the mountains."

Sotaesan said, "You will receive karmic retribution for this action in the future." Chongsinhaeng was so ashamed when she heard Sotaesan's words that she began sweating and her face turned red. So she quickly went down to the creek and repeatedly splashed water on her face. She told everyone to do the same. Sotaesan said, "That is not how you wash your face!"

Chongsinhaeng asked, "Then how do we do it?"

Sotaesan said, "You must scoop the water like this." Sotaesan carefully scooped the water into his hands, turned away from the creek, and washed his face. Then he said, "Even if water is free and abundant, we should use it sparingly, and not waste it. If people use water wastefully, they can be born in a place where water is hard to attain."

64

Fluctuating Good and Evil

Sotaesan always told his students, "Even if a person has wronged, he can change through true repentance and effort. The murderous and evil energy in him will disappear and be replaced with warmth, and his future will be brightened. However, even a person who has done good deeds in the past can at times be filled with unwholesome energy. If he holds on to resentment and harmful intentions, his future will inevitably be darkened."

65

How a Cat Raises its Kittens

Sotaesan said, "Once when I was in Youngkwang, I saw a cat raising her three little kittens. I watched every day and noticed how wise she was in raising her babies. I realized there were aspects of her methods that were better than some of our human methods. At first, when she gave birth, she embraced her kittens, fed them regularly, licked them, cleaned them, and took care of them with utmost devotion. If a human came close, the mother would stare back at the human instinctively to protect her babies from any harm.

As the babies grew up, the mother would go outside and kill a mouse to feed them. Sometimes the mother would catch one alive and bring it home, let it go and then catch it again with her paws in order to teach the kittens. Every day the mother would play with a mouse in different ways and eventually kill it for the kittens, teaching them how to hunt and feed themselves. After those initial lessons, the mother denied the kittens any of her milk, and only caught mice for herself. She no longer brought any mice home. If any of the kittens begged for milk or tried to nurse from her, she would simply refuse. This encouraged the kittens to be independent. How could I not think that this cat was better than many human beings?

In another instance, I was in a Won Buddhist temple in Seoul, and saw a cat raising its two kittens in the storage room in a house in Changshin District. I noticed that one kitten was well-fed and healthy, while the other one was very thin and weak. I asked why, and Kim Sammaehwa replied, 'Upon birth, the two kittens were of the same size, however, when the mother stopped giving them milk, only one of them became independent and was able to feed on its own. The other one continued to expect the mother to bring food and was unable to catch a single mouse on its own. But the mother, instead of being sympathetic, ignored it so the kitten started to starve.' A human mother would be extremely sympathetic and try to help the starving child, but in the case of a cat, the mother is detached and holds no exception. I think that this naturally teaches the kittens independence.

How wise is this? An ignorant person would think that loving their children is letting them do whatever they want, raising them to be lazy and delinquent. They could learn a thing or two from these cats. Even though they came from the same womb, one cat grew up to be independent and self-reliant, while the other one remained dependent and rejected. Why do you think this is?

Both animals and humans follow certain rules of behavior. To be independent one must have a storage chest full of merit and happiness. By contrast, being dependent on others inevitably results in suffering. This applies to both cats and humans, which should be sincerely considered throughout our lives."

66

A Bird is the Same as You

Palhyeon, the son of Kwon Tonghwa, one of Sotaesan's students, became very ill. Someone mentioned that eating boiled birds could heal him, and told his father to take the bird's nest full of baby birds from the clothing repair room, and boil them for his son. Kwon Tonghwa asked Sotaesan what he thought about this.

Sotaesan replied, "How could you be a practitioner of the dharma, and be so unaware?" Sotaesan was so dumbstruck that he was silent for a long time. At last, he spoke again, "The bird's mind is no different from yours. Your love for your son is no different from the bird's love for its young. How would you feel if the bird took your child and ate him?"

67

Wishing for the Future

February 5th, 1926 was Lee Kongju's thirtieth birthday. A celebration took place at her home. Sotaesan arrived with Park Sasihwa and Lee Sungak to wish her a happy birthday. Sotaesan asked Lee Kongju, "What do you wish to do in the future? What would bring you the most satisfaction?"

Lee Kongju answered, "I wish to fight for the rights of women in Korea. So first, I wish to study literature in Japan, come back and write books to enlighten the women of Korea."

Sotaesan said, "Your wish to enlighten thousands of women in Korea is a great and admirable idea, however, the women of Korea are only a small part of the billions of people in this world. The fact that you are thinking only of the women of Joseon is too narrow-minded. You said you wanted to write for women; there are only a handful of women who are literate. How about expanding your horizons, to become a master of ethics and help the entire human race?"

From that day on, Lee Kongju started dreaming of a different life. And her faith in Sotaesan grew even deeper. Whenever Sotaesan came to Seoul, she would bring him to her house and listen to his lectures. She even took care of his traveling expenses during his stay. Eventually, her house became a formal evening lecture hall.

68

Making Communal Decisions

on Your Own

When Oh Changgon was in Youngsan, someone wanted to sell him land. He saw that the man offered him a price much cheaper than its actual worth. He thought he should return to Won Buddhism Headquarters and discuss the matter with everyone, but there was no time. So he bought the land by himself and returned. He believed that Sotaesan would praise him for making such a bargain, so he proudly said, "Master, we decided to buy some land in Youngsan. The price is less than half of the market rate. I believe it will be a huge profit for our order."

"I see. When did we discuss buying land?"

"There was no time, so I signed the contract on my own and am reporting to you now."

"You made a communal decision on your own. Do you realize what you have done wrong? If you make such decisions by yourself just for the sake of profit, who knows what will happen to our order in the future? Someone might betray us and sell a part of our community for personal gain. Go back right now and revoke the contract. Pay the deposit if you must. Such wrong ideas must be eradicated early."

So, he went back, paid the deposit and revoked the contract.

69

An Angry Mind

Sotaesan said, "The anger you have can never be understood by others. That anger is caused by blame and resentment because you cannot control your mind. If you wish to make controlling your mind your primary focus, then you must first learn to be grateful."

70

The Eyes of Wisdom

One day, Sotaesan was with officer Hwang Ichon in the office of the Head Dharma Master. He asked, "Ichon, you don't know me, do you?"

"Of course I do. You are Master Sotaesan."

"That is not what I mean. You do not recognize who I truly am. You only see me through your physical eyes. You have to open your eyes of wisdom to really see me."

71

Just Let it Be

One day, Sotaesan scolded Song Tosung. The reason was that Song Tosung had seen a bird caught in a spider's web and he tore it open to set the struggling bird free. Tosung thought, "Why does this puny spider dare to eat a bird this big?"

Sotaesan told him, "Tosung! Why did you interfere in something that is not your business?"

"I set the bird free because it was struggling, unable to fly because of the spider web. Was I wrong?"

"Do you think you were right? That spider built the web for days and nights so that it could catch something to eat. Think of how the spider will hate you for setting the bird free."

"What should I have done?"

Sotaesan said, "Do not interfere—just let it be."

72

The Living Universe

Sotaesan spoke of the origins of the universe. "The universe is filled with energy that constantly moves—and it is aware. The universe has nothing that is truly dead. Listen carefully. I will give you an example: The boils on your body let out pus. This is because the flesh around it is rotting. You may think that the smelly, disgusting pus has no place in this world. You may think the same about excrement. You may say that excrement does not contain any life, since it is the leftovers of what we have already digested. However, these things are never dead, nor should they be left just to rot. They may seem dead, but the elements inside them are alive. Let's say you use the pus and the excrement as fertilizers for cabbages or radishes. Then the plants will grow more abundantly than those without fertilizers.

If the pus and excrement were truly dead without any living power, then the plants would not have grown well. They may seem rotten and dead to us, but they are actually alive. And this life-force transforms into food for plants. That is why even though the pus and excrement may change form and disappear over time, their vital energy continues on. So we can conclusively say that nothing in this universe is ever truly dead. This universe is filled with living energy. That is how the universe changes and renews itself."

73

Dried Fish

Kim Yongsin from the Busan Won Buddhist temple, once told the Master Sotaesan, "Teacher, I am afraid to go to funerals."

Sotaesan asked, "Yongsin, are you afraid of dried fish?"

"No."

"Dead people are no different! What are you so afraid of?"

She said nothing in reply. From then on, Kim Yŏngsin would mutter to herself about dried fish every time she went to a funeral.

74

The Foolish Servant

In Youngkwang, there lived a servant named Mongbau. One day, his master told him, "You should go to the Jangswong market this morning."

"Yes sir." said Mongbau, and so he went to the market. Later on that day, his master wanted to tell him what kind of errands to run at the market, but he was nowhere to be found. Finally in the afternoon, Mongbau came back. His master asked, "Where have you been?"

Monbau answered, "I have been to the market."

"But I never told you what to buy at the market."

"But you told me to go this morning."

Sotaesan used Mongbau as an example never to act without reason or questioning.

75

A Crooked Il-Won-Sang, a Round Il-Won-Sang

Sotaesan showed his students a crooked Il-Won-Sang and a round one. "Which one looks better?"

They answered, "The round one. The crooked one does not look very good."

Sotaesan said, "That is right. When we use our minds, we must be like the round Il-Won-Sang and not the crooked one."

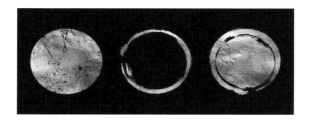

76

Servants Who Cried Without Reason

There lived a politician who had many wives. Because of the many wives, there were many family members and as a result, many deaths and funerals. Following tradition, the servants cried aloud all day, but they never really knew who died. Their actions were meaningless and impractical.

After telling this story, Sotaesan said, "The politician's servants were wearing clothes and eating food that the citizens had worked so hard for. To waste their precious time in this world so meaninglessly is almost a crime. People who behave this way have no reason to live here. Therefore, always be alert, always have a purpose and look back on your life every morning and every night. You cannot live life without a useful purpose."

77

The Two Pheasants

One day, Sotaesan went to the market in Youngkwang with Kim Kwangson. While he was resting at a house, he asked the owner, "Is there not a lady of this house?"

The owner replied, "Whenever I married, the woman left after just a few months. So I live alone."

Sotaesan, upon hearing this, smiled and said, "If I find you a good woman, will you live with her?"

The owner gladly agreed and said, "If you do so, I will be very grateful."

While Sotaesan stayed in that house, he watched many people come and go from the market. He saw a woman, called to her and said, "Do you have a husband?"

She replied, "No, I am a widow now."

Sotaesan said to her: "Would you consider living with the owner of this house?" The woman was taken aback and refused at first, but after meeting the owner, she seemed to be willing. Sotaesan sat in front of the couple, and offered to share a story, "Once upon a time, a couple of wild pheasants were living happily in the mountains. When they died, they were reborn as good people, but they struggled to find each other. They spent half their lives wandering alone, without children. When they finally found each other, they reunited as a couple and finally led a joyful life together."

As he was finished with the story, the owner and the woman were crying as if they had lost a parent.

Sotaesan said, "That is why it is crucial to form positive affinities with people. Remember this!"

Sotaesan left the house. On his way from the market, he told Kim Kwangson, "Did you understand what I told the couple today? They were pheasants in previous lives, and they cried so hard when I talked about their past. People live through many lifetimes, but forming good affinities with others is the most important blessing of all."

Part 4

SEARCHING FOR TRUTH

78

Inquires of a Young Boy

On a clear spring day, when Sotaesan was seven years old, he went up to Ongnyo peak to look at the sky. "Such a clear blue sky. I wonder how far and high it is? How is it so clear? I wonder how far it goes. Who lives at the end of the world?"

When he was nine years old, he began to ask questions about life. "What do people live for? Where do they go when they die? How was I born into this world? Why are there rich, poor, noble, lowly, handsome, ugly, good and bad people, even when they are all human beings? What am I?" As he began to question these things, his inquiry into the truth was deepened.

79

What is a Noble Person?

This story took place after the death of Sotaesan's father, Park Seongsam. During his life, Park Seongsam was indebted to a few people, so Sotaesan ran a business to earn money.

After three months, he went into town to visit a rich man to pay the debt. When Sotaesan walked in, the rich man was wearing a traditional hat and was speaking to a guest. Spotting Sotaesan, he said, "You must be Seongsam's son. Are you here to pay your father's debt?"

Sotaesan, who was twenty-one at the time, paid his respects and sat down. In a stern tone, he said, "Seeing as you are rich and have many responsibilities in the government, I thought you would be a nobleman. But now I see that you are no different than a commoner. Our households had a friendly, trusting relationship, which is why you lent us money. However, after my father's passing you never even stopped by. Instead, you talk about money the first chance you get."

Sotaesan threw the bag of coins he had strapped to his waist, in front of the rich man, and it landed with a loud thud. "I have paid my debt." said Sotaesan as he stood up to leave. The rich man felt ashamed and could not lift his head. All his servants, who had gathered around to see what the commotion was about, were also left speechless.

Sotaesan marched out the front door without another word.

80

Standing Still

Before Sotaesan attained great enlightenment, he was working as a seller at the market. On a hot summer day on his way to the market, he stopped under a zelkova tree to cool off, eventually going straight into a state of deep meditation. The men who were supposed to meet with Sotaesan went to the market on their own after he failed to appear.

When they were returning after the day's work, they found Sotaesan still standing like a statue under the tree. "What are you doing here?" asked one of the men. Sotaesan did not reply. He was so still that they could not tell if he was alive or dead. The men started to shake him. "Wake up! What are you doing?"

After a few shakes, Sotaesan opened his eyes and looked around. "Where is this place? What time is it?"

"It's Sunjin-po, and the sun has almost set."

"Really? What am I doing here?"

"That is exactly what we want to ask you. Why are you asking us?"

"I do not know. Why am I here?"

"Think hard, my friend."

Sotaesan stared at the men for a while, and then finally said, "I remember now. I was on my way to the market and stood under this tree to cool off. I was watching the clouds go by. I must have been standing here all day."

81

NON-Distraction

One day, before Sotaesan had attained enlightenment, he was meditating on a rock near a small house, when a young woman approached him with a basket of herbs at her waist. She would not leave even after the sun began to set.

Seeing her reluctance to leave, Sotaesan asked, "Where did you come from? Why will you not go home?"

She replied in an embarrassed, yet earnest tone that she had seen him before and could not help but fall in love. She begged him not to leave her.

Sotaesan said, "There are strict rules between a man and a woman. I am studying, and it would be a distraction."

The woman did not listen to his stern words. Finally, Sotaesan told her, "Perhaps there are other people around this area. I will go check and come back." He went to another nearby mountain, sat on a rock and went into a deep meditation. The woman waited for him, but eventually she grew tired and returned home. Sotaesan returned to the original place and retrieved some water from a nearby spring. He cleaned the place where she had been sitting and continued to meditate.

82

The Prayer

Yi Wonhwa helped Sotaesan when he was practicing attaining great enlightenment. One day, Sotaesan became ill, but still continued to meditate facing a wall. Yi Wonhwa became concerned and said, "What are you doing? Are you trying to become a governor?"

Sotaesan said to Yi Wonhwa, "A governor is not very important. I want to be a great teacher like Zhuge Liang."

"Wash yourself in cold water in the morning, and at night, concentrate with your mind and pray for me."

So, Yi Wonhwa washed herself twice a day, regardless of the weather. She put a bowl of clear water on a rock, bowed in eight directions, and prayed. "Divine spirits of heaven and earth, please make this man a local governor."

Sotaesan saw this and asked, "I am very thankful that you are praying for me, but why do you pray that I should be a governor?"

She responded, "He is the most powerful man I know."

Sotaesan said, "It is a very high position. But if you are going to pray for me, pray that I will be the man to deliver all the people in the world." From that point on, Yi Wonhwa prayed for him to be the savior of the world.

83

The Teacher and the Founding Master

In Youngkwang, the birthplace of Sotaesan, there was a teacher named Kim Hwacheon, who was eight years his senior and was known for his literary skills.

Sotaesan had visited Kim Hwacheon to learn the Chinese characters. After Sotaesan attained great enlightenment, he wished to have students of his own. So, with Buddhist scripture in hand, he revisited his old teacher. The whole town was already aware of Sotaesan's enlightenment. However, Kim Hwacheon still thought Sotaesan to be ignorant due to his illiteracy.

The young Sotaesan approached Kim Hwacheon and asked, "Teacher, could you read and interpret this book that I have brought you?" Kim Hwacheon was slightly startled by the Buddhist scripture. After sifting through a few pages, he became alert and attentive. He said, "I have seen Confucian books, but I am unfamiliar with Buddhism."

"Then read the letters to me, and I will translate."

Kim Hwacheon agreed, and started reading. He came upon a word written in Hindi that he was not familiar with. "I have no idea what this word is."

The once illiterate Sotaesan who always took off to the mountains instead of studying, started reading the rest of the text without effort, interpreting the book with utmost ease. The teacher was frozen in shock.

84

The Man who Carried Sotaesan on His Back

On a warm summer day, after Sotaesan attained great enlightenment, he was walking with Yi Sunsun when they came upon an old man. The old man saw Sotaesan and stared at him in awe.

Then he asked, "Young man, where are you from?"

After Sotaesan replied, the old man offered to carry him on his back. He explained, "I have met many people over several decades, and have seen their fortune through their faces. However, I have never seen a person of your stature, build, and demeanor. I would like to get to know you, which is why I am offering to carry you on my back."

That day, the old man led Sotaesan to a nearby hut, treated him well and praised him endlessly.

85

The Strong Man who was Scolded

When Sotaesan and his nine disciples started the reclamation work, they would offer townspeople construction work and pay them a fee in return, however, many would sneer and laugh. "You can't trust Sotaesan and his students—they are too poor. Recently, their so-called leader could not even maintain his own household, and none of his students are exceptional. Right now, they are carrying out the reclamation project. Pretty soon they will realize their efforts will come to naught, and they will begin fighting among themselves. In the end, they will all split off in different directions."

At this time, in a nearby town, there was a man who was known to be very strong. One day, this man became drunk and told everyone, "My friends, I will go to their construction site tomorrow and make fools out of them all!" The next day, this man brought a few friends to the construction site and told Sotaesan, "We came to work. I am several times stronger than most men."

Sotaesan said, "Work hard, and I will pay you plenty of money."
The man was stronger than three men put together, and, just as he had bragged earlier, he began to taunt Sotaesan. Instead of listening to Sotaesan, he would pour dirt in the wrong place. He planned to pick a fight with Sotaesan when he was being scolded. However, Sotaesan knew this man's plan, and would only watch. Then suddenly he struck the strong man's backpack with a stick and shouted, "You imbecile! You rely on your meager strength. Who are you trying to fool?"

The man was shocked. The blood drained from his face, and his limbs became stiff. As he stood like a statue, Sotaesan said, "Take this man over there and let him rest."

After a long time, the man recovered as if he had come out of a coma. "Am I dead or alive? Where am I?"

His friends, who had come to work along with him said, "How could a strong man like him lose his mind from just a scolding?" After this incident, the man redeemed himself by working several times harder than all the rest. No one came to the construction site to make fun of the project anymore.

86

What Should We Do?

After Sotaesan attained great enlightenment, he was working on a reclamation project with his students.

At that time, the Political Independence Movement of March 1st ignited all over the country, and his students asked him, "Master, everyone is fighting for independence right now. As people who have lost our country to Japan, what should we do at this point?"

Sotaesan replied, "This Independence Movement is more than a fight against Japan's oppression. It is the call for our nation's enlightenment. It is a bell urgently calling for the dawn to come. Right now, we are very busy and our time is limited. Everyone in the world has a calling in this lifetime that requires adequate timing. During a turbulent time, such as this, we must think about that calling. Right now we must hurry to finish this project and start praying to the divine spirits."

87

Our Buddhas

When Sotaesan resided in the Won Buddhism Headquarters, some people came to say hello, and asked him, "Where have you enshrined your buddha?"

Sotaesan replied, "Our buddha is outside right now. Wait a while if you wish to see him." The group did not understand this and considered it quite odd. A while later, at lunch time, the workers came in from the fields with farming tools on their backs.

Sotaesan pointed to them and said, "These are the buddhas of our community." The people became even more confused.

88

The Old Woman who Went Back Home

An old, wealthy woman with many children came to the Won Buddhism Headquarters to meditate. After a week, she paid a visit to Sotaesan before leaving home. "If I leave my house, none of my sons or daughters-in-law will even notice if the spices, or firewood is stolen from my storeroom. I cannot free my mind and concentrate on my meditation any longer. I must go back home."

After she left, Sotaesan told his students, "A person's obsession is so terrifying. She has tied her mind with an invisible string, and it is dragging her to her own prison. A physical prison in this world is breakable, but one can never escape the prison of your own mind, not even in the next life. If you are so obsessed with your wealth and household, once reincarnated, you will always be born near your old house. If you had good human affinities in your previous life, perhaps you will be reborn as a person, otherwise, you may be born as an animal or an insect. It is a terrible, fearsome thing. A person should let go of their attachments and obsessions before leaving this world. This is the most crucial thing."

89

The Reason Why He Did not Cure Her

One day, a female Won Buddhist member in her fifties came to greet Sotaesan. She looked hesitant as if she had something troubling her, and finally she said, "Master, I have been suffering with heartburn for years. Please tell me the remedy." Sotaesan told her that she had come to the wrong place.

"That is an illness of the physical body. Go see a doctor or a pharmacist—I cannot do anything for you." But the woman kept asking him for the remedy. Sotaesan continued to refuse her.

After she left, Hwang Ichon said to him, "You are a very stubborn man."

Sotaesan smiled. "Do you think so?"

Hwang Ichon replied, "I will tell you a trick for next time. Take dried pumpkin leaves and hand them to the next member who asks you for medicine. They will believe the pumpkin leaves will actually work and get better. Even if they don't, the leaves are harmless. If you charge a small amount for each bag of the leaves, it will cure their illnesses and you can make a little money on the side."

"You have a point. If I give them medicine that cures their illness, they will look up to me even more, however, when this happens, I will no longer be a teacher of spiritual practice, but a simple drug peddler.

90

The Prayer on the Train

K im Yongsin was escorting Sotaesan by train from Seoul to Won Buddhism Headquarters in Iksan. When Sotaesan stepped in, everyone in the train stood up for him. No matter where he went, people would step aside to make way for Sotaesan. Whenever he got on a train, he would take a seat and close his eyes for a silent prayer. Kim Yongsin was curious, and asked, "Master, why don't you talk with the people next to you?"

"I am praying that this train gets to its destination safely."

Kim Yongsin kept this in mind and from then on, whenever she rode a train, she always prayed.

91

Cleaning the Train Bathroom

Sotaesan boarded a train for Seoul with a student. As the train passed Daejeon, Sotaesan stood up to go to the bathroom. When he did not return after a long time, the student was worried, so he went to the bathroom. Just then, Sotaesan stepped out. "Master, what took you so long?"

"I was cleaning the bathroom."

"You were cleaning the bathroom?"

"I walked in and it was dirty. I feel that during the Japanese occupation, the Japanese would say that Koreans are so inferior and ignorant that we don't even know how to use the bathroom, and that is why we lost our sovereignty to them. During a difficult time like this, we must be even stronger and even more able to defend our nation's pride and honor."

92

Failing the Buddha Test

When Sotaesan was visiting Seoul, all the residents heard that the living buddha was coming, and so they gathered to see him.

They became disappointed and left after seeing Sotaesan's unexpected human like aspects. At lunch time, lettuce and other food was served. Sotaesan quite enjoyed it. When the people saw him, they thought, "What buddha enjoys food so much?"

Sotaesan visited the bathroom after his meal. The remaining people thought, "We have been fooled!' and ran away.

When Sotaesan returned to the Won Buddhism Headquarters in Iksan, he told Hwang Ichon, "Ichon! I went to Seoul and failed the buddha test. Even a person better than I, would have failed. Everyone ran away from me!"

93

Japanese Surveillance and Difficulties for Won Buddhism

When Won Buddhism was introduced to the world, and the Order became increasingly organized, the Japanese surveillance became stronger. Whenever Sotaesan moved locations, there were undercover policemen following him. Kim Yongshin described that time in this way:

Whenever Sotaesan came to Seoul, we led him to a house in Gyedong. Upon his arrival, all the members in Seoul would gather there. Lee Tongjinhwa would wear a pretty, blue skirt and bow gracefully. Kim Sammaehwa would also bow sincerely to Sotaesan. Aunt Lee Kongju would wear a fashionable head covering as well as Western clothes. I would always stand behind Sotaesan to fan him. While all these ladies entered the building to listen to Sotaesan, we never knew that there were Japanese policemen spying from a small hill behind the house.

Then one morning, we discovered that Sotaesan had disappeared. He left to go to Iksan without telling anyone. I thought about how strange this was as I was packing my bookbag to go to school. Then, a Japanese detective came in to search the house, "Who was that man yesterday?"

"Him? He is my uncle."

I answered in fluent Japanese. Whenever someone asked this question, I always said he was my uncle. My mother and aunt would say he was their brother, and my grandmother would say he was her nephew.

94

To Clean is to Study

One day, Sotaesan happened to pass by, and asked one of the girls, "Your parents are paying for you to study here at the Won Buddhism Headquarters. Why are you working instead of studying at a desk? Is that not going against their will for your education?"

One of the girls answered, "I am studying right now."

Sotaesan asked, "How can you study while you are working?"

One girl replied, "To sit down and study, like you say, is to study the ethical philosophy. However, working is to use that knowledge in real life."

Sotaesan responded, "You are right. In the past, practitioners of the Way would often waste their time memorizing scriptures but would not carry out that knowledge. Scriptures are like signposts. True practitioners of the Way do not stare at the signpost, they actually follow the sign and go on their way along the path. You have chosen the correct way in your studies."

95

Have You Become a Buddha?

K im Gwanjung would visit the Won Buddhist temple and meditate often. If he had questions, he would ask great Buddhist masters.

One day, he asked Sotaesan, "Does an enlightened person exist, even in a chaotic world like this?"

Sotaesan replied, "In a world like this, do we not need many enlightened persons?"

Kim Gwanjung asked again, "Then Master, have you become a true buddha?"

Sotaesan smiled and replied, "I realize the karmic principle of cause and effect. The biggest sin in this world is to pretend to be enlightened when you are not, and thereby to interfere with many people's futures with this lie. I could establish this religion because I know this principle. Becoming a buddha cannot be achieved through talking or listening. You need to reach a certain level of awakening to clearly recognize a practitioner's degree of awaking. The value of true dharma will be proven by future generations."

96

Even Buddha Cries
Because He is Human

One of Sotaesan's first nine disciples was Kim Kichon. He was the first disciple in Won Buddhism whose awakening was acknowledged by Sotaesan. When Kim Kichon was working as a minister at the Busan Won Buddhist temple, he became very ill and passed away. The news of his passing reached the Won Buddhism Headquarters at Iksan, causing everyone living at the Headquarters to rush to the Great Enlightenment Hall at 5:00 am. Sotaesan was also there. Everyone was sitting quietly in the completely dark hall, when Sotaesan started to weep. At that moment, everyone else started to cry loudly.

This was not the only instance where Sotaesan showed tears. When Kim Kwangson—his uncle and student—passed away, and when Yi Tongan (founder of Bohwa-dang, a herbal medicine shop) passed away, Sotaesan also cried. He always shared his grief with the public, however, his sadness never lingered, and he moved on with his tasks.

Sotaesan's son passed away at the age of nineteen. He could not bear to be with his son during his last moments, and he left the room. That afternoon at 2:00 pm, he gathered his students and gave a lesson about life and death. He was a buddha, who could give a dharma lecture just three hours after his son's death. He did not let the pain or sadness drag him down because he knew how to control his mind.

97

After a Plane Ride

Sotaesan said, "One time, Changgi convinced me to travel by airplane, so I got on an airplane for the first time. When I entered the plane, they had us put cotton balls in our ears and gave us a pen and paper with which to communicate. I was sitting across from Changgi, and there were three Japanese soldiers sitting next to me. When the plane began to take off, the propeller was spinning very loudly. I looked down and felt like I was in a flimsy bamboo basket, and became very nervous. I told Changgi to be at ease, and I myself closed my eyes and went into meditation. I was determined not to have my faith or meditation shaken; even if the plane broke down and I fell with it to my death. Once I had this thought, I became peaceful.

After a while, Changgi shook me and showed me a piece of paper telling me that we had almost arrived. His face was very pale. A short while later, we landed safely at Mokchunpo airport, and finally arrived at Bohwa-dang.

Whenever we do something for the first time, we are filled with confusion and worry, however, with strong faith and determination to achieve something greater, there is no need to have fear or worry. No matter what tragedy strikes, a person with such a mind cannot be shaken. So whenever you are confronted with distractions or disturbances, do not be perturbed. Instead, always keep your faith and remember how to calm your mind. Not only will your fears and pain subside, you will even be able to remain calm in the face of death. Faith is truly a great thing.

98

You Should not Waste Dirt

Kim Bongsik was cleaning the yard, and had gathered some dirt and dust with his broom. He put the dirt and dust in a sack, and was on his way to the dumping ground when Sotaesan called from his room, "Who is there? What are you carrying?"

Sotaesan walked out of his room and said, "Pour it on the ground. Don't you see that you have gathered all this dirt and not just the dust? This dirt was paid for. You cannot be wasteful with this." He sorted the dirt out by hand and poured it into a hole where the rain had washed the dirt away. He hardened the soil with his feet by patting it and stepping on it.

99

The Police Station

Sotaesan told police officer Hwang Ichon, "I have been to the Gimje police station, and they just had me sit down. Honestly, I had done nothing wrong. It is not a crime to help people. Ichon, the police station is a very nice place."

Ichon asked, "What made you think it was so nice?"

"Think about it. When I stayed there, even though there was very little food, I was still fed three times a day. They gave me water when I was thirsty, they let me sleep at night and woke me up in the morning. Paradise was not far away. I do not understand why people are so afraid of that place."

Ichon said, "Master, that is not a good thing."

Sotaesan said, "If you are guilty, you will become afraid of your own bedroom, let alone a police station."

Won Dharma Publications
Won Dharma Center
361 Route 23, Claverack, NY 12513
www.wondharmacenter.org

You can contact us at 518-821-2150 or
info@wondharmacenter.org